YOUR KNOWLEDGE H

Carsten Lietz

Was German expansionism which led to World War II simply an extension of the war aims of 1914-18?

GRIN Verlag

Bibliografische Information der Deutschen Nationalbibliothek:

Die Deutsche Bibliothek verzeichnet diese Publikation in der Deutschen National-
bibliografie; detaillierte bibliografische Daten sind im Internet über http://dnb.d-
nb.de/ abrufbar.

Imprint:

Copyright © 1995 GRIN Verlag GmbH
Druck und Bindung: Books on Demand GmbH, Norderstedt Germany
ISBN: 978-3-640-67097-0

This book at GRIN:

http://www.grin.com/en/e-book/6000/was-german-expansionism-which-led-to-
world-war-ii-simply-an-extension-of

GRIN - Your knowledge has value

Der GRIN Verlag publiziert seit 1998 wissenschaftliche Arbeiten von Studenten, Hochschullehrern und anderen Akademikern als eBook und gedrucktes Buch. Die Verlagswebsite www.grin.com ist die ideale Plattform zur Veröffentlichung von Hausarbeiten, Abschlussarbeiten, wissenschaftlichen Aufsätzen, Dissertationen und Fachbüchern.

Visit us on the internet:

http://www.grin.com/

http://www.facebook.com/grincom

http://www.twitter.com/grin_com

University of Bristol
Department of Historical Studies
Course: The Making of Contemporary Europe, 1870-1994

Essay topic: German Expansionism

Was German expansionism which led to World War II simply an extension of the war aims of 1914-18?

By Carsten Lietz

"I recognise that Powers will be Powers. (...) The vital question, it seems to me, concerns Great Britain and France. They were the victors of the first World war. They had the decision in their hands. It was perfectly obvious that Germany would seek to become a Great Power again; obvious after 1933 that her domination would be of a peculiar barbaric sort."[1]

[1] A.J.P. Taylor: The Origins of the Second World War, foreword

TABLE OF CONTENT

The Problem

The Aims of War

Ideologies and Origins

Before the Wars Began

Conclusion

1. The Problem:

Were it only the exceptional ideas and plans of Adolf Hitler and his NSDAP that led to World War II or did the Führer only succeed in the old aims of German foreign - and in the end - war policy of the former empire? If yes, it would not be only Hitler's war, but a German war which could not be reduced any longer to the Nazi-ideology, but to a constant German policy, independent of the political system until the end of World War II.

It has to be explained, which aims Germany followed in World War I and World War II, why it followed them, who supported these aims in Germany and why, and of which kind their aims's ideological background was.

2. The Aims of War

The main aims can be distinguished in territorial and technical aims. In World War I, German territorial war aims included in the West parts of France, especially the expansion of the German part of Alsace-Lorraine, which was supposed to be regained in World War II, the economical important area of Longwy-Brie with large iron ore deposits, the occupation of Belgium, Holland and Luxembourg. These aims were nearly identically with Hitler's aims in World War II.[2] Already in his book „Mein Kampf", written in 1924, Hitler complains, how dangerous - in his opinion - the French policy was for Germany[3] :

"Für Deutschland jedoch bedeutet die französische Gefahr die Verpflichtung, unter Zurückstellung aller Gefühlsmomente dem die Hand zu reichen, der, ebenso bedroht wie wir, Frankreichs Herrschgelüste nicht erdulden und ertragen will." ("But for Germany the French threat means the obligation, to put back all emotional moments and to shake everybody's hand, who is as threatened as we are and not willed to endure and to bear France's thirst for power)[4]

In September 1914 German chancellor Bethmann Hollweg had explained the war aims in the West in a very similar way:

---

[2] F. Fischer: Der erste Weltkrieg und das deutsche Geschichtsbild, p. 364
[3] For the usability of "Mein Kampf" as a source, see Trevor Roper, pp31-32; W. Maser, pp.117-120 & 139.
A.J.P. Taylor sees in the Lebensraum-idea in Mein Kampf admittedly no war-plan and doesn't regard Mein Kampf as a blueprint of Hitler's later aims, but accepts the Lebensraum-idea as a constant topic in Hitler's (and other right-wing politician's) aims. (The Origins.., Second Thoughts-foreword)
[4] A. Hitler: Mein Kampf, p. 705, my translation.

France had to be weakened, so that it will not be able to recover as a great power. [5]

In the East, Germany wanted to turn Poland into a satellite state and to completely occupy a large area at the border. Also the Baltic States should later on be integrated in the Reich, although they were promised to Russia in the Hitler-Stalin-Pact. In the South-East, Turkey was expected to end in strong economical and political dependence of the Reich both in World War I and II. Also similar were the aims in the Balkan area: Serbia was occupied in both wars. [6]

So only one important territorial aim of 1914 was not resumed in World War II: Hitler pursued nearly no colonial aims like the German Central-Africa-Plan of the Kaiser's government in World War I, although tactical reflections about possibilities of colonial winnings can be found in Mein Kampf. [7]

Added to these main territorial aims was a technical aim in World War I for the West and the East: An economic leadership of Germany in central Europe, *"including France, Belgium, Holland, Denmark, Austria-Hungary, Poland (!), and possible Italy, Sweden and Norway"* [8]. Bethmann Hollweg's government developed the "Program of a Central European Customs Association", in which a German leadership should be established to *"stable Germany's economical predominance in Central Europe"*. [9] And so did Hitler. [10] Also

[5] Bethmann- Hollweg's War Aim Programm of Sept. 9th 1914, in: F. Fischer: Geschichtsbild, p. 156
[6] F. Fischer: Geschichtsbild, p. 366
[7] A. Hitler: Mein Kampf, p. 690
[8] Programm eines mitteleuropäischen Zollverbandes, in: F. Fischer: Geschichtsbild, p. 157, my translation
[9] Programm eines mitteleuropäischen Zollverbandes, in: F. Fischer: Geschichtsbild, p. 157, my translation
[10] A. Hitler: Monologe, p. 57

comparable were the plans to clear eastern territories like the
Ukraine of their inhabitants and to resettle Germans.[11]

---

[11] Trevor-Roper p. 44/45; A.J.P. Taylor, Hitler: Monologe, pp. 55 & 70

3. Ideologies and Origins

But were the origins of these aims as similar as the aims itself?   At least the constitutional situation and majority proportions in the Reichstag, the German parliament, were different: The monarchy of World War I was replaced by the Weimar Republic which changed to the   Third Reich and instead of the old Empire's centre-conservative government under Bethmann Hollweg the fascist NSDAP regime lead the country.

But even though the NSDAP was established after the end of World War I, and Hitler himself as Führer, chancellor and supreme commander of the armed forces   as a lance-corporal had been in no remarkable function during World War I, especially in its first years the decisions of government and army-command of the Third Reich were still influenced by some of the powerful groups of former Empire's times. Even Hitler's own thoughts and speeches referred frequently to German political failures around World War I.[12]

Conservative and nationalistic politicians of the former German leadership like Ulrich von Hassel (ambassador in Italy until 1939), supported Hitler's first official war aims of the years 1938-1940. They wanted to reestablish the borders of 1914, but not to fight Russia and a new World War.[13] But instead of the old Bismarck-borders Hitler had a *Großdeutschland* in mind, which included all areas with German speaking population.

What were the grasps at world power in 1914, was the Lebensraum-motive of 1938, which also was a commonplace of

---

[12] see A. Hitler: Mein Kampf, vol. 1 („Eine Abrechnung") and Monologe im Führerhauptquartier

its time.[14] But different from 1914, for Hitler's regime the strong anti Semitic and anti Bolshevik ideology was even more important than the desire of being a world power. This aim was just the result of the Nazi-ideology. While Bethmann Hollweg's government carried the nationalist umbrella to unite opposite political groups, supporting the *Weltpolitik* for different reasons, Hitler followed his world-view of the German master race, the Jewish threat and the eastern subhuman creatures.

It is controversial discussed, if *Mein Kampf* was a blue print of Hitler's later on policy and warfare or just a document of his ideas. But it is fair to say that there is broad agreement about his constant way of thinking from *Mein Kampf* until his death 1945. Reading *Mein Kampf* or the Table Talks during wartime 1941-1944 shows that it is obvious that the racist ideas formed the base of Hitler's war aims and his grasps for world power , which he had already announced in *Mein Kampf.* : "Unterdrückte Länder werden nicht durch flammende Proteste in den Schoß eines gemeinsamen Reiches zurückgeführt, sondern durch ein schlagkräftiges Schwert."[15] A war for the German liberty was his way not only to cancel the territorial statutes of the Versailles treaty, but also to win the space the "German master race" would need.

In the Empire *Weltpolitik* was the government's answer to internal problems without specific aims since 1897. Under this umbrella the chancellors von Bülow and later Bethmann Hollweg tried to bring opposite groups together: Conservatives agreed to the *Weltpolitik's* anti-Polish policy, heavy industry profited from the Navy Laws for the construction of new ships.

---

[13] Trevor-Roper, p. 40
[14] A.J.P. Taylor: Origins, Second Thoughts foreword
[15] Hitler: Mein Kampf, p. 689

9

But hopes of expansionistic organisations like the Pan-German-League or the Navy League had been disappointed: The *Weltpolitik* did not have that strong effects to make all lacks of interior cooperation unrelevant.[16]

Until 1917 nearly all important political groups stood together in the war policy: Alldeutsche, Conservatives, National-Liberals, Zentrum, the Social Democrat's right wing and the high command. In the beginning of the war, the Kaiser's and chancellor's concept of the nationalist *Burgfriede* (political truce) seemed to be successful: "I know no parties anymore, only Germans", declared Wilhelm II at the Reichstag in August 1914.[17]

But each of the applauding parties was following different interests. Most of the Social Democrats wanted to fight the tsarist regime and combined ethical imperialism with economical interests, the industrial leaders within the National Liberals hoped for a weakened England and industrial areas both in Belgium and France, the Zentrum-party was - partly for theological reasons - particularly interested in Poland and Lithuania. [18] Main conflict between the parties was about the concept of *Siegfriede* (peace of victory) that Bethmann Hollweg had already proclaimed in his September 1914 programme[19]. Conservatives demanded further expansion, while the majority of the Social Democrats preferred a mainly defensive character of the war. Nevertheless, a small group of SPD-imperialists, led by Lensch, Haenisch and Kolb, saw in World War I a war for social change. They were looking for, what many aristocrats were afraid of: Concessions from the monarchy to the socialist

---

[16] Kaiser, p. 449
[17] Carr p. 212
[18] Fischer: Geschichtsbild, p. 155-156
[19] see p. 2, footnote 5

movement and the abandonment of the Empire's status quo
monopoly of political power. [20]

---

[20] Carr p. 215/216

4. Before the Wars Began

In public opinion as in government the believe in a need to expand globally, to get Germany's "place at the sun", with more and stronger colonies rose already in the first decade of the twentieth century. Chancellor Bethmann Hollweg was considering a possible war to win the French Congo and was supported by public opinion, the majority of the press, the Conservatives and National Liberals in the Reichstag.[21]

In domestic policies the situation was getting worse and worse for Bethmann Hollweg. Getting along very well nor with the Conservatives neither the Socialists his *policy of the diagonal* made him increasingly dependent on the Kaiser and his aristocratic advisers.

Abroad the situation was getting tenser since the Balkan war between Italy and Turkey began in September 1911, especially after the Balkan states entered the fights in October 1912. The following defeat of the Ottoman Empire caused a serious threat to Austria-Hungary and its Habsburg-monarchy in Vienna. First Germany and Russia worked together at the Conference of London to avoid war, which would have probably been involved both countries, which had not been rearmed at that time. But when the Balkan states went to war again in 1913, Bethmann Hollweg's government and Wilhelm II assured Austria Germany's assistance in forcing the Serbs out of Northern Albania. Just a few months before a new army bill had passed the Reichstag to raise the German army strength from 663.000 in 1913 to 800.000 in 1914. Also France and Russia were rearming. In February 1914 the Russian government

---

[21] Kaiser, p. 465

wanted to transform the Entente into a strong alliance to prevent any German threat to Russia, after a German general was in command of the first Turkish army corps to reorganise the weakened troops after the war. The German reply was very harsh: The Kaiser stated Russia to be an enemy.[22]

Hitler's first steps leaving the path of Stresemann's former conciliatory policy were done with support by army command and foreign office: Germany left the League of Nations, rearmed secretly, built up a German air-force until 1935. All this was tolerated by France and especially Britain, although there were some half-hearted diplomatic protests. His first intolerable blow against the Versailles treaty was the reoccupation of the demilitarised Rhineland in March 1936. But France already feared the German military strength and did not intervene. Again Hitler had only to face diplomatic protests from London, Paris and the League of Nations. 1937 Italy joined the Anti-Comintern-Pact, the Rome-Berlin-Tokyo-Axis was established. The powerless League of Nation counted for little, the European countries returned to a balance-of-power-policy towards Germany, Belgium declared her neutrality in 1937. In the East Czechoslovakia remained the only French ally after Rumania had left the French defensive system and Bulgaria, Yugoslavia and Italy bound themselves together. In this November 1937 situation Hitler explained his leading staff in the Hossbach-conference, the Lebensraum problem had to be solved by 1943-1945.[23]

Comparing the German policies before both wars shows that both times the governments were following long termed aims, even though certainly not each decision was precisely planned. Main difference is in the interior situation: While Bethmann

---

[22] Carr, p. 204-206

Hollweg had to deal with a weakened state, Hitler was head of an efficiently working regime which had complete control of Germany.

---

[23] see Carr, p. 340-347; Taylor, Second Thoughts

5. Conclusion

It was not simply nationalist expansionism that led Germany to World War II like it did at World War I. While the Empire's government mainly aimed to raise a system of German predominance in Central Europe and to establish Germany as a world power with a strong Central African colony, the Hitler-government tried to expand German territory and influence not only for a grasp at world power or economical reasons, but to fulfil the demands of its own racial ideology. By preparing the end of Czechoslovakia, the reoccupation of the Rhineland and forcing the *Anschluß* of Austria, Hitler did what other strong chancellors could also have done. But the origins and long-termed aims of his policy were different. So Germany's aim in World War II was not only extension of the aims of World War I, they were a new interpretation of Germany's role in the World.

Bibliographic references:

A. Bullock: Hitler - A Study in Tyranny, London 1964, 2nd edition

W. Carr: A History of Germany 1815-1990, London 1991, 4th edition

F. Fischer: World Policy, World Power and German War Aims, in: The Origins of the First World War, ed. by H. W. Koch, London 1984, 2nd edition

F. Fischer: Der erste Weltkrieg und das deutsche Geschichtsbild. Beiträge zur Bewältigung eines historischen Tabus, Düsseldorf 1977

I. Geiss: Origins of the First World War, in: The Origins of the First World War, ed. by H. W. Koch, London 1984, 2nd edition

A. Hitler: Mein Kampf, München 1936, 176th-177th edition

A. Hitler: Monologe im Führerhauptquartier 1941-1944. Die Aufzeichnungen Heinrich Heims, ed. by Werner Jochmann, Hamburg 1980

J. Joll: The 1914 Debate Continues: Fritz Fischer and his Critics, in: The Origins of the First World War, ed. by H. W. Koch, London 1984, 2nd edition

D.E. Kaiser: Germany and the Origins of the First World War, in: Journal of Modern History, Aug. 83

A. Kuhn: Hitlers außenpolitisches Programm - Entstehung und Entwicklung 1919-1939 (=Stuttgarter Beiträge zur Geschichte und Politik, ed. by M. Greiffenhagen, E. Jäckel, A. Nitschke, vol. 5), Stuttgart 1970

W. Maser: Hitler's Mein Kampf - An Analysis, translated by R.H. Barry, London

A. J. P. Taylor: The Origins of the Second World War, London 1963

J. Thies: Hitlers „Endziele": Zielloser Aktionismus, Kontinentalimperium oder Weltherrschaft?, in: Nationalsozialistische Außenpolitik, ed. by Wolfgang Michalka (=Wege der Forschung, vol. 297), Darmstadt 1978

H. R. Trevor-Roper: Hitlers Kriegsziele, in: Nationalsozialistische Außenpolitik, ed. by Wolfgang Michalka (=Wege der Forschung, vol. 297), Darmstadt 1978

H.-U. Wehler: Das Deutsche Kaiserreich 1871-1918, (=Deutsche Geschichte, vol. 9, ed. by J. Leuschner), Göttingen 1975, 2nd edition